STEAM ON SHED
BORDERS STEAM
LIGHT RAILWAYS
standard gauge and narrow gauge
OF BRITAIN
ARTICULATED LOCOMOTIVES OF THE WORLD
MAIN LINE STEAM
STEAM IN
india
GREAT WESTERN
STEAM THROUGH THE YEARS
MIDLANDS
WESTERNS
THE WELSH NARROW GAUGE
SUPERPOWER STEAM
AROUND THE WORLD
BRITISH TRAMS
SCOTTISH
BRANCH LINE STEAM
THE MIDLAND RAILWAY
the later years of
LMSR LOCOMOTIVES
GREAT WESTERN
a pictorial history
SOUTHERN
STEAM IN ACTION
SCOTTISH RAILWAYS
in the heyday of steam

DIESELS WEST

DIESELS WEST

G. F. GILLHAM

D. BRADFORD BARTON LTD

With the famous Westbury White Horse standing out clearly in the background, Class 50 No.50013 *Agincourt* smokes its way westward near Fairwood Junction with the 15.30 Paddington-Penzance on 16 September 1978. The semaphore signal on the left was taken out of use two days later and replaced by the colour light signal visible behind the train.

 2973/BL *ISBN 0 85153 364 7*

printed in Great Britain by Lovell Baines Print Ltd., Newbury, Berkshire
and bound by Western Book Co Ltd., Maesteg for the publishers

D. BRADFORD BARTON LTD · Trethellan House · Truro · Cornwall · England

introduction

In 1972, the Western Region inter-city scene was still much as it had been for years, the only change on the motive-power side being the withdrawal of most of the diesel-hydraulic classes and their replacement by a smaller number of diesel-electrics transferred from other Regions. Twenty-year-old Mk.1 coaching stock was still in use on many main line trains, which were themselves running to timetables scarcely improved since the introduction of diesel traction twelve years before.

But gradually, year by year, this scene was to change dramatically. Starting in 1973 with the introduction of air-conditioned stock on some South Wales workings, and continuing with the arrival of the English Electric Class 50s from Midland Region in 1974, the prototype High Speed Train trials in 1975 and the last year of the 'Western' diesel-hydraulics in 1976, Stage 1 was completed in May 1977, when a full HST service was introduced to both Bristol and South Wales. Stage 2 was due to commence in 1980-81, when these trains would take over the West of England services from both Paddington and the North, so ending a long history of locomotive-hauled trains to the West.

One notable feature of these changes has been the widespread disruption and diversions caused by the massive track-relaying programme, especially on the Bristol and South Wales routes, where many miles were completely re-aligned. Together with this, power re-signalling schemes have replaced many mechanical signal boxes – and this process is continuing, with the aim of abolishing semaphore signals on the main line to the east of Plymouth by 1981.

To many Western Region enthusiasts, the introduction of the HST has destroyed much of the interest and variety of recent years, and the disappearance of the traditional signalling is just another step towards a 'unified' railway system – which, though doubtless efficient and hopefully profitable, will be sadly lacking in atmosphere.

The photographs in this book have been chosen to illustrate the changes that have been taking place on the routes to the West during the years 1972-78, and show many scenes already gone – as well as those due to vanish over the next few years.

Class 53 No.12 00 *Falcon* moves the 10.45 to Weston-super-Mare away from Paddington station on 16 June 1972. This unique locomotive was built for experimental purposes by Hawker Siddeley (Brush) Ltd. in 1961 and was in many ways the prototype for the later Class 47 design. After extensive trials on British Railways, it was purchased by them in 1970, numbered 1200, and allocated to Bristol (Bath Road). *Falcon* was finally withdrawn from service in October 1975.

On a wet and cold evening in December 1977, platforms 9 and 10 at Paddington play host to Nos.50 022 and 47 089 *Amazon* which had arrived on the 14.35 from Bristol and the 11.05 (FO) from Penzance respectively.

Class 52 No.1028 *Western Hussar* hurries the 06.35 Penzance-Paddington past West Ealing on 20 September 1974, passing Class 35 No.7018 waiting to leave the up yard with an engineers' train for the Greenford loop. No.7018 was one of the last three of the 'Hymeks' to remain in service, being withdrawn in March 1975, and has subsequently been preserved.

Class 50 No.50 033 passes the motive power depot at Southall on 20 May 1975, at the head of the 13.45 Paddington-Bristol. This depot was the last in the London area to service WR steam locomotives – until December 1965 – since when it has been used as a stabling point for diesel multiple units.

On a fine May morning in 1975, Class 47 No.47 035 sweeps past the E M I factory at Hayes with the 06.35 from Penzance.

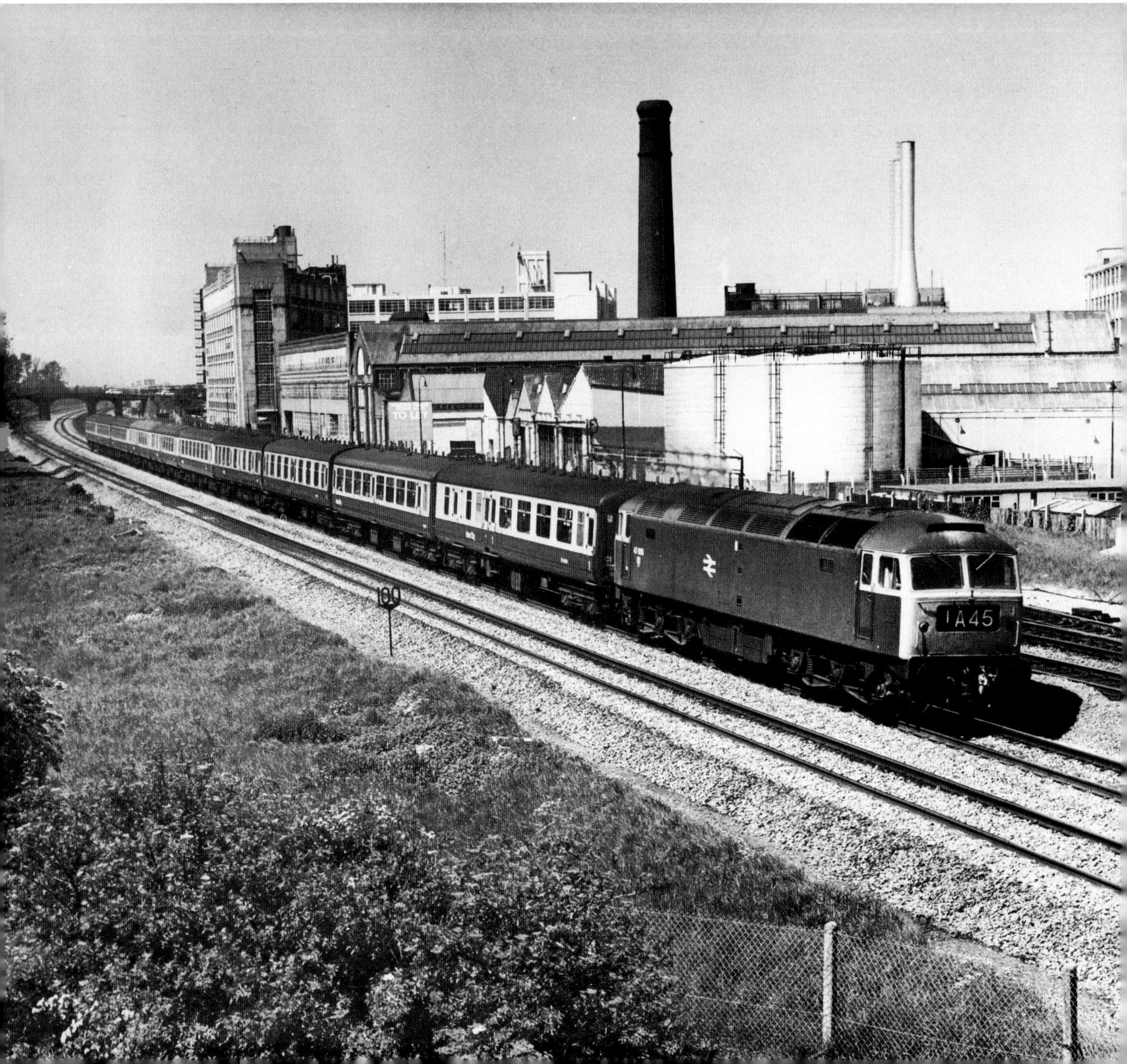

The summer of 1974 saw the first regular appearances of both the Class 50 locomotives and air-conditioned stock on Western Region, as in this view of No.50 027 working the 09.45 from Weston-super-Mare through Iver on 6 August.

When the Class 35 diesel-hydraulics were withdrawn in 1974-75, their first replacements on the Worcester-Hereford services were some Class 31s, recently transferred from Eastern Region. On 20 May 1975, No.31 230 passes Slough with the 08.08 from Hereford.

To all Western Region diesel enthusiasts, the best-known headcode was probably 1 B45, the down 'Cornish Riviera Limited'. On 8 October 1975, just three months before headcodes were abolished, the train was worked by No.D1072 *Western Glory*, seen here near Ruscombe.

Carrying an express freight headcode, No.D1048 *Western Lady* runs through Twyford on 18 May 1974, with a train of parcel vans.

Because of a motive power shortage on Western Region in 1973, the 'Westerns' were given an extended lease of life, and some of the most run-down received an overhaul and repaint at Plymouth Laira depot. One of the first to be re-done in this way was No. D 1033 *Western Trooper* which had just been returned to service when photographed working the 12.30 Paddington-Paignton through Sonning Cutting on 26 April. The front of the locomotive bears evidence of a patch having been welded on to repair some minor accident damage.

The introduction of the High Speed Trains in 1976 released some Class 47s and 50s to work with the Worcester and Hereford services, on which the newly-rostered Class 31s had found it difficult to keep time. On 23 July, No.50 049 accelerates away from Reading with the 08.08 from Hereford.

A busy scene at Reading early in January 1975 as Class 50 No.50 026 and the 09.30 Bristol-Paddington are held at the up platform, to allow Class 47 No.47 069 to overtake with an up excursion from Plymouth.

The north side of Reading station is often busy with parcel traffic, as here on 19 April 1973, with both Class 35 No.D 7016 and Class 47 No.16 92 (47 104) working short parcel trains.

When the separate Southern Region station at Reading was closed in September 1965, an extra platform was laid in on the south side of the WR station, together with a spur to connect with the old Southern route. On a sunny May day in 1978, a Waterloo train departs from the new platform as No.50 038 *Formidable* approaches with the 13.30 Paddington-Penzance.

During the last few months of locomotive-hauled workings to South Wales, No.47 484 *Isambard Kingdom Brunel* makes an energetic start away from Reading with a Paddington-Swansea train. Note the anonymous headcode – a common sight in the period between their abolition and the fitting of the now-common marker lights.

The years 1974 and 1975 saw the 'Western' diesel-hydraulics having their final fling on the Birmingham line, where they had last worked regularly in 1964. On 24 April 1975, a rather scruffy and run-down No.D1016 *Western Gladiator* wheels the 12.25 from Birmingham towards Goring and Streatley.

n a fine spring day in 1973, Class 35 'Hymek' No.D7017 trundles a short mixed freight own the relief line near Pangbourne. This locomotive was one of the last of the class to e withdrawn, and has been preserved by the Diesel & Electric Group on the West omerset Railway.

The English Electric Class 50s were the first locomotives on WR to have a maximum speed of 100 mph, and this was used to the full when recovering from the numerous temporary speed restrictions caused by the widespread track upgrading of the mid-70s. On 24 April 1975, No.50026 and the 14.15 Paddington-Bristol come off the long four-track embankment across the Thames Valley near Cholsey and Moulsford.

22 Another Paddington-Cardiff working, the 09.15 down, disturbs the peaceful Wiltshire countryside between Shrivenham and Swindon, as Class 47 No.1586 (47 463) accelerates away at full throttle from a temporary speed restriction.

With the gradual introduction of air-conditioned stock on the South Wales services from 1973 onwards, the use of the 'Westerns' rapidly declined until, by 1975, they were occasionally seen only on the Cardiff semi-fast workings. One such was the 13.15 down, seen here leaving Didcot behind No.D1040 *Western Queen* on 25 August.

1C28

No.50010 hurries the 10.45 Paddington-Bristol past the lines of scrap wagons and coaches at the rear of Swindon Works on 8 June 1976. This was once the site of Rushey Platt Junction, and the siding leading off to the right is all that remained of the connection to the former Midland & South Western Junction line, and its station at Swindon Town.

Wootton Bassett Junction, just west of Swindon, is the point where the Bristol and South Wales routes diverge, and it is the latter that Class 37 Nos.37 142 and 37 236 take with a train of empty private-owner stone hoppers, later on the same day. Shortly afterwards, Class 47 No. 47 483 restarts the 14.05 from Cardiff away from a signal check at the approach to the junction.

On 17 August 1976, Class 47 240 heads eastwards out of Bristol (Parkway) station, with the 10.25 Taunton-Manchester. Opened in May 1972, this was the first station on BR to be built next to a motorway to attract the long-distance motorist, and has been so popular that the idea has been repeated elsewhere.

On the same day, the 08.08 Newcastle-Bristol was worked by 'Peak' No.45 055 *Royal Corps of Transport*, seen here approaching the station from the east.

Class 47 No. 47 512 starts a Swansea-Paddington train away from Parkway station, and passes Class 31 No.31 205 as it runs into the down yard with a short freight.

In April 1973, during the last few months of regular 'Western' working on the Swansea services, No. D1029 *Western Legionnaire* (with a red background to its number and nameplates) curves away from Severn Tunnel Junction with the 13.00 from Paddington.

On a windy May day in 1972, Class 45 No.12 (45 011) eases past the start of a temporary speed restriction at Magor, between Severn Tunnel Junction and Newport, while working the 08.24 Manchester-Cardiff.

37206
N
627

ince their introduction in 1962, English Electric Class 37s have had a monopoly of all oal and mineral workings in South Wales and, although the distances worked are not reat, the combination of heavy loads and steep gradients in the area often tax these ocomotives to their limit. Seen opposite is a typical South Wales working, as No. 37 206 reeps through Newport station with a train of empty mineral wagons.

Recent years have seen an increase in the number of direct services from South Wales to the North of England, one example being the 11.45 Cardiff-Newcastle, seen here leaving Newport on 7 April 1978 behind Class 45 No.45 062.

One of the few passenger services on Western Region to be regularly worked by the Sulzer Class 25 diesels has been that from Cardiff to Crewe; on 30 August 1978 No.25 224 passes Rumney, near Cardiff, with the 11.30 up train.

A busy scene at Swansea on 27 September 1972, as Class 47 No.1932 (47 493) arrives with the 11.00 from Paddington, while Class 08 shunter No.4174 (08 944) waits to remove the empty stock of a previous arrival. The forest of fine lower-quadrant signals disappeared in October 1973, when this area was taken over by the new Port Talbot power box.

1A43

1C27
47 484

While High Speed Trains now have a monopoly of the Bristol line services, it was still possible on Sundays during 1978 to see locomotive-hauled trains here, for on these days the West of England line was closed for engineering works and all trains diverted via Bristol. On a sunny Sunday in May, No.50 049 *Defiance* curves down towards Corsham with an afternoon Paddington-Penzance train.

Returning to the Bristol line, these two photographs were taken at Thingley Junction (near Chippenham) in August 1975, while the South Wales direct line was closed for engineering works – all trains being diverted via Bath and Bristol. Above, No.D1051 *Western Ambassador* has a train of Mk.1 stock on the 08.42 from Swansea, while (below) Class 47 No.47 484 *Isambard Kingdom Brunel* passes in the opposite direction with the 09.40 from Paddington. The branch to Melksham can be seen diverging at the right.

With the waters of the Kennet & Avon Canal in the foreground, the 14.35 Bristol-Paddington, headed by an unidentified Class 50, nears Bathampton on 28 March 1977 – just five weeks before the introduction of full HST services on this route.

Earlier on the same day, the morning Bristol-Paddington parcel train, normally a Class 31 or 47 working, is seen on the climb away from Bath behind Class 46 No.46 006.

After taking over from a Midland Region Class 45, Class 52 No. D1037 *Western Empress* awaits departure from Bristol (Temple Meads) with the down 'Cornishman' on 29 April 1970.

Class 46 No. 46015 restarts a Severn Tunnel Junction–Plymouth freight away from Temple Meads in April 1978, after a short stop to change crews.

When BR ended the practice of carrying a headcode on locomotives in January 1976, the empty panel was in some cases used unofficially to display an abbreviated locomotive number – in this instance, Class 50 No.50 008 had become 5008, as it waits to leave Temple Meads for Weston-super-Mare.

The branch from Thingley Junction, Chippenham, to Trowbridge lost its regular passenger services in 1966 and was reduced to single track, but it has been kept open since then for through freight workings. On 2 March 1974, No.D1052 *Western Viceroy* curves onto the branch at Thingley with a Swindon-Westbury train of stone empties.

As well as being used for freight traffic, the branch is also useful as a diversionary route — as in March 1978, when the West of England line was closed for the remodelling of Newbury station; No.50043 is nearing Melksham, with the 09.21 Paignton-Paddington.

Just a few weeks after its transfer from Midland Region, No.50 002 hurries the 07.53 from Paignton through Theale on 14 May 1974. The 'bus shelter' on the up platform does not seem to harmonise very well with the rest of the GWR architecture.

In its last few months of service, No.D 1062 *Western Courier* nears Ufton Crossing, near Aldermaston, with the 10.30 Paddington-Paignton in May 1974. No.D1062 has since been preserved by the Western Locomotive Association, and is housed on the Severn Valley Railway.

Moving on to the West of England main line, the first landmark after leaving Reading is Southcote Junction, where the Basingstoke line diverges. On 29 April 1976, the down 'Cornish Riviera Limited' approaches the junction behind an unusually clean and well-kept Class 50, No.50 011. The section of line from here down to Castle Cary has always been known as the 'Berks and Hants' route – an odd title, as the line never comes within 30 miles of Hampshire.

1A39

1B35

1A55

One feature of the 'Berks and Hants' line which does not make it ideal for high-speed working is the almost continuous series of curves – No. D 1053 *Western Patriarch* rounds a typical example near Aldermaston with the 09.55 from Paignton.

A lightweight duty for Class 35 No. D 7093 in May 1974, as it leaves Newbury with three container wagons for Colthrop siding, just up the line. Note the semaphore distant signal and fogman's hut on the left – both rapidly disappearing features nowadays.

The 'Golden Hind' was introduced in 1964 as a prestige service from Plymouth, and originally ran with specially selected stock and locomotives, but over the years it has lost its distinction, and is now just the first train of the day up from Penzance. The name, however, has been retained, and the train is seen here hurrying through Newbury on a sunny April morning in 1975, behind Class 50 No.50 024.

The first station to the west of Newbury is Kintbury, which is still open for local passenger traffic, although the goods yard in the foreground was removed in 1965; here No. D1021 *Western Cavalier* disturbs the peace and quiet as it rushes through with the 12.26 (SO) Paddington-Penzance on 8 September 1973.

One of the last weekday workings to the West to go over to air-conditioned stock was the 10.40 to Plymouth, photographed a few weeks before the change, approaching Hungerford behind No.47 484 *Isambard Kingdom Brunel.*

Hungerford was noteworthy for its fine variety of ex-GWR signals, which lasted until July 1978, when the area was taken over by an extension of Reading power box. Above, Class 50 No.50 002 passes he signal controlling the entrance to the down goods loop with the 06.50 Plymouth-Old Oak empty vans on 16 February 1977, while (below) No.D1015 *Western Champion* is seen working a 'Senior Citizens' excursion o Newquay past he other end of the oop on 29 April 976.

Between Kintbury and Savernake, the 'Berks and Hants' line runs close to the Kennet & Avon Canal, and the combination provides some fine locations for photography. Above, Class 47 No.47 236 is seen near Great Bedwyn heading for Paignton in August 1976, while (opposite) No.50 049 *Defiance* rushes the down 'Cornish Riviera Limited' through the adjacent village of Little Bedwyn in May 1978. The canal on this stretch is gradually being restored, and will eventually be open for pleasure craft throughout its length.

A waiting passenger gets a wave from the driver of No.47 098 as it slows for the stop at Pewsey on a June evening in 1976. The train, from Paddington to Westbury, is a commuter service, and stops at all stations between Reading and Westbury.

Skirting the edge of Salisbury Plain, No.D1015 *Western Champion* trundles a Theale-Westbury empty stone train past the daffodil fields at Manningford, near Pewsey, on 27 April 1973.

Making good time with its light load, No.D1053 *Western Patriarch* hurries a relief to the 08.35 Penzance-Paddington through the remains of Patney and Chirton Junction station on Easter Saturday 1975. This was once the railhead for the Devizes branch, closed in April 1966.

With the temperature still well below freezing, Class 47 No.47512, at the head of the 12.30 to Paignton, kicks up a trail of powdered snow as it approaches Woodborough on New Year's Day 1979.

1B35
50 004

On a frosty November morning in 1974, the 10.30 Paddington-Paignton curves through avington behind Class 50 No.50 004, which is unusual in that it carries no BR emblem.

On Sunday mornings during the summer of 1974, both the main Bristol and South Wales lines were closed for engineering work connected with the introduction of the High Speed Trains, and this meant that the few trains that did run were diverted via the 'Berks and Hants' line to Westbury, and then round the little-used east curve to Bristol. On 16 June, Class 47 No.47 501 comes off the curve at Hawkeridge Junction, with the late-running 09.15 Paddington-Swansea.

YEOMAN

ıe fine ex-GWR junction signals at the north end of Westbury station are probably the ›st-known on the West of England line and have figured in many published photographs. ıcing them on 21 June 1976, No.50 027 has the road for Paddington with the 07.53 ɔm Paignton, while No.47 036 waits to follow with a stone train for Theale.

With the usual bevy of diesel enthusiasts waving from the front coach, No.D 1056 *Western Sultan* brings the 10.05 Weymouth-Bristol into Westbury on 16 October 1976. The mechanical signalling at this end of the station was replaced when the layout was altered in September 1978.

With the decline in Welsh coal traffic in the late 1970s, a few of the numerous English Electric Class 37 diesels allocated there were found to be surplus to requirements, and were moved to other WR areas where suitable work could be found for them. Westbury, with its large number of heavy stone trains, found them very useful, and on 12 September 1978 Nos. 37 291 and 37 295 approach the station with a 50-wagon load from Merehead stone terminal.

The avoiding line round Westbury station was opened by the GWR in 1933 and, although no shorter than the original route, it avoids the speed restriction and congestion in the station area. Above, No.D1041 *Western Prince* sweeps the 06.35 from Penzance round the bypass in June 1975, while (below) Class 47 No.1609 (47030) approaches Fairwood Junction with a down train from Paddington in March 1973.

A chance meeting of two ex-works locomotives at Fairwood Junction, as Class 33 No.33 205 approaches with a train of ballast hoppers from Somerset Quarry, and passes No.46 026 *Leicestershire and Derbyshire Yeomanry* heading for Merehead with empty ARC stone wagons. Note the new colour-light signal waiting to be brought into use next to the semaphore junction signal.

Seen through the signals at Clink Road Junction, near Frome, Class 50 No.50 042 speeds the down 'Cornish Riviera Limited' westward on 23 September 1978. This locomotive was named *Triumph* soon after this photograph was taken.

During a three-week period of engineering work at Westbury in September 1978, all West of England services due to call there were diverted, making a rare appearance at Frome instead. Class 50 No.50 038 *Formidable* and the 10.30 to Plymouth look somewhat out of place here under the original broad-gauge wooden roof – a unique feature now happily to be preserved.

Witham, Somerset, was once the junction for Wells and Yatton but, although the branch was closed to passengers in 1963 and the station itself in 1966, the stone traffic from Merehead Quarry on the branch means that the signal box is busier than ever. On a sunny April morning in 1976, No.D1033 *Western Trooper* passes the site of the station with the 06.35 from Penzance.

Class 31 No.31 295 comes off the Weymouth branch at Castle Cary and passes between two fine ex-GWR signals with a train for Bristol on 4 April 1974. The unusual signal on the right is a 'backing' signal, used for controlling reversing moves from the up platform, and was probably one of the last examples to remain in use on Western Region.

outhern Region Class 33 diesels are occasional visitors to the West on inter-Regional eight workings – one such being the Fawley-Tiverton Junction oil train, seen here rolling rough Castle Cary behind No.33 029 on 2 July 1975.

On a crisp April morning in 1974, No.D1068 *Western Reliance* heads an up train from Plymouth away from Taunton and across the sedge moors near Langport.

Taunton remains one of the last strongholds of the semaphore signal on WR, and bo these views were taken here on 21 April 1976. Above: Class 46 No.46 005 restarts t 11.15 Plymouth-Manchester away from the station while, below, the 10.30 fro Paddington passes the junction with the goods lines to the east of the station behi Class 47 No.47 226.

47 226

Deep in the heart of the Somerset countryside, Whiteball Tunnel marks the summit of the long climb from both east and west over the Blackdown Hills, and in the days of steam provided a stiff test for both locomotives and crew. Nowadays, however, it is the sharp curves more than the gradient which restrict the speeds, although heavy freights still occasionally require banking assistance. On 11 August 1978, No.50 048 *Dauntless* has just left the tunnel, and starts the long descent towards Exeter with the 12.23 Paddington-Penzance, while (opposite) No.45 039 *The Manchester Regiment* storms the last section of 1 in 115 from the west, while working a Penzance Liverpool express earlier the same day.

Class 47 No.47 438 passes the empty platforms at Tiverton Junction on its way to Paignton on 30 May 1974. Since the branch lines to Tiverton and Hemyock closed in the early 1960s, the station here has been a shadow of its former self, with just a handful of main line trains calling each day.

On a crisp November morning in 1973, No. D1049 *Western Monarch* then in its last few months of service, coasts past Cowley Bridge Junction and prepares to stop the 09.30 Paddington-Penzance at Exeter (St. Davids).

Working a Plymouth-Bristol parcels, Class 47 No.47 286 waits for the right-away at Exeter (St. Davids) during a November evening in 1978.

The low winter sun casts long shadows at the west end of St. Davids station, as No.50 007 arrives on the 09.55 Paignton-Paddington. On the right, facing in the opposite direction but also bound for London, No.33 023 waits with the 12.25 to Waterloo.

The one line to the west which will not be worked by High Speed Trains is the former Southern route from Waterloo to Exeter, but these two photographs are included to show the diesel power which has worked these services so far. When steam finished in 1964, Western Region supplied as replacements the Class 42 'Warship' diesel-hydraulics, and these popular locomotives worked all trains until they too were withdrawn in October 1971. The view above shows No. D831 *Monarch* approaching Buckhorn Weston Tunnel, near Gillingham, with a train of Mk.1 stock from Waterloo on 23 February of that year. Since 1971, the service has been in the capable hands of Southern Region Class 33 diesel-electrics, and (opposite) No. 33 008 climbs away from Wilton on the single-track section to Gillingham, with the 17.00 from Waterloo, on a fine August evening in 1978.

62

Back on the West of England main line, the stretch between Exeter and Teignmouth is well known for its fine sea views, sharp curvature and speed restrictions. The first two of these are evident in this photograph, as Class 50 No.50 045 skirts the small harbour at Cockwood, near Starcross, with an afternoon Penzance-Paddington service in June 1976.

During the summer of 1976, a local shortage of diesel multiple units required several Plymouth Division local workings to revert to locomotive haulage. One example was the 19.30 Exeter-Paignton, seen here passing Dawlish Warren behind Class 25 No.25 223 on 21 June.

20

After a signal check, Class 47 No.47 086 *Colussus* accelerates the Stoke-St. Blazey empty clay wagon train through Dawlish station on 22 June 1977.

During recent years, one feature of trains to the West has been the increase in the number of Motorail services, many of which now run all through the week during the summer months. One such is the 19.30 to Stirling, seen here waiting in Newton Abbot station behind No.47 199. As the carflats are shunted on to the rear, No.47 063 passes through with an up oil tank train.

Class 50 No.50 002 comes off the well-known sea wall section and prepares to stop the 14.30 from Paddington at Teignmouth on a sunny May evening in 1977.

By 1972, the few remaining Class 42 'Warship' diesel-hydraulics had been mainly relegated to freight workings, and only on summer Saturdays might a sight like this be seen – No. D 805 *Benbow* nearing Aller Junction, with the 09.25 (SO) Manchester-Penzance train.

Coasting round the curve at the foot of Dainton bank, No. D 1058 *Western Nobleman* passes Aller Junction signal box with a short parcel train from Plymouth on 10 July 1974.

In the days of steam, a 50 mph speed limit on a gradient of 1 in 46 would have been rather optimistic, but it gives an indication of just how much speeds have increased in recent years. On 18 July 1973, Class 46 No.155 (46 018) heads the 09.15 Liverpool-Plymouth up past Stoneycombe siding, and on towards Dainton summit.

Just a short distance from the previous photograph, Dainton bank has steepened to 1 in 36, and Class 47 No.1989 (47 287) works hard as its twelve-coach Edinburgh-Plymouth train approaches the tunnel portal on a warm July evening in 1973.

The driver of No.47 244 has his cab window open on a warm August day in 1975, as his locomotive curves through Totnes with a short Class 7 coal train bound for Plymouth.

7B3
W

Dead on time at 12:43, No.47 258 brings the up 'Cornish Riviera Limited' into Plymouth station on 24 June 1976. Here the restaurant car section will be added before departure for Paddington some eleven minutes later.

A few moments after the photograph above was taken, the 09.30 from Paddington rolls in at the other end of the station behind No.50 003, still immaculate after a recent general overhaul.

With the temperature in the eighties, the sun beats down on Liskeard station as green-liveried Class 47 No.1935 (47 257) arrives with the up 'Cornishman' on 13 July 1971.

Passing the milk depot on the left, No. D1034 *Western Dragoon* approaches the level-crossing at Lostwithiel with the 08.00 Bristol-Penzance on a July morning in 1974.

Class 46 No.46 002 provides unusual motive power for the 12.40 Penzance-Paddington, as it skirts the coast at Carlyon Bay, near St. Austell, later the same day as the scene above. Deputising for a failed Class 50, this locomotive would probably only have worked the train as far as Plymouth.

The Newquay and Falmouth branch lines are now the last in the West of England to enjoy through main line services on summer Saturdays, while the former also boasts a through train to Leeds on Fridays, seen here waiting to depart behind Class 47 No.47 230.

There has always been a heavy parcels and mail traffic to and from Penzance, and as the 13.05 to Leeds arrives at St. Austell on 1 September 1972, the first three of the eight coaches are parcel vans. The locomotive is No. D1046 *Western Marquis*, which will work this train as far as Bristol.

Working a train of empty china-clay wagons from Fowey, Class 25 No. 7505 (25 155) crosses over to the St. Blazey line outside Par station on a sunny July day in 1972. These ocomotives were transferred from Midland Region earlier that year to replace the withdrawn Class 22 NBL diesel-hydraulics, and have since handled most of the short-haul freight and clay workings in the area.

With its twin Maybach engines at full power, No.D1045 *Western Viscount* accelerates the late-running down 'Cornish Riviera Limited' through the remains of Gwinear Road station on 17 July 1974. This was once the junction for the Helston branch but this closed in 1962, the station itself surviving only another two years.

Four months after it was transferred to Western Region, Class 50 No.50 007 brings the 16.10 from Penzance up the short 1 in 61 gradient near Angarrack, between Hayle and Gwinear Road.

Still looking smart after a recent repaint at Laira depot, No.D1030 *Western Musketeer* nears Marazion with the daily parcels train from Paddington and Bristol. This stock will spend the day at Penzance before departing eastwards again at 15.22

After a fine morning, storm clouds build up over Penzance on 17 July 1974; Class 47 No.47159 waits to depart at 12.40 on the 305-mile journey to Paddington, which will be reached at 18.40.

1A45

All is quiet at Penzance on a sunny September evening in 1972, as an immaculate Class 52, No. D1065 *Western Consort,* stands at the head of a departure for Manchester.

MIDLAND
OF THE BORDER
STEAM
GREAT WESTERN
STEAM MISCELLANY
BODMIN AND WADEBRIDGE
BR STANDARD STEAM
IN ACTION
BRITISH
NARROW GAUG
STEAM
GREAT WESTERN
BRANCH LINE STEAM
DIESELS
ON SCOTTISH REGION
BR DIESELS
IN THE
LANDSCA
BR DIESELS
IN ACTION
BRITISH
H.C. CASSERLEY
in the heyday of steam
SOUTHERN 188
THE LYNTON & BARNSTAPLE RAILWAY
ROPEAN
TEAM
ERN
MOTIVE
THE WARSHIPS
THE
WAINWRIGHT
STEAM
NORTH EASTERN
STEAM
N ACTION
LONDON MIDLAND
STEAM IN ACTION 4
42/43 DIESEL-HYDRAULICS
THE
LONDON
RT
BUS
UTHERN
STEAM
STANIER 8F
2-8-0
GREAT
CENTRAL
recalled
GEORGE DOW